TEMPLATE-FREE®
S·T·A·R·S

Jo Parrott

That Patchwork Place®

Acknowledgments

My sincere appreciation goes to:

Mary Jane Brooks for her continued help and support—never has there been a more understanding and helpful assistant;

Audrey Couvillon for doing so much machine quilting in such a short time;

Mary Ray for hand quilting the 1,000 Pyramids and the Alabama Star;

Anita Kienker for testing some of the patterns;

My mother, Verniece Snow, for binding them;

Dana Parrott, my daughter-in-law, for her machine quilting and proofreading;

Brenda Rinehart, my daughter, for introducing me to the "Guide to Rapid Revision";

Nancy Martin and her staff for taking my rough draft and primitive drawings and turning them into a beautiful book.

Dedication

To my partner in life and in business, Henry Parrott. I could not get as much done as I do without his help and consideration. He has spent Monday nights watching football on a small black-and-white television in the back room, has eaten more take-out food than a man should have to, and has learned to smile and help out behind the counter in our shop when it is necessary. His patience with me is second only to his patience with our grandchildren. Thank you, Henry, for sharing your life with me.

Template-Free® Stars©
© 1993 by Iva Jo Parrott

That Patchwork Place, Inc.
PO Box 118
Bothell, WA 98041-0118
USA

Printed in the United States of America
98 97 96 95 94 93   6 5 4 3 2 1

Credits

Editors — Ursula Reikes & Barbara Weiland
Copy Editor — Liz McGehee
Text and Cover Design — Kay Green
Typesetting — ArtWorks
Photography — Brent Kane
Illustration — Nicki Salvin-Wight

Library of Congress Cataloging-in-Publication Data

Parrott, Jo.
    Template-free stars / Jo Parrott.
        p. cm.
    ISBN 1-56477-024-9 :
        1. Patchwork—Patterns. 2. Patchwork quilts. 3. Stars in art.
    I. Title.
    TT835.P364 1993
    746.9'7—dc20   92-21194
                                                                              CIP

✳✳✳

Table of Contents

INTRODUCTION

The second quilt I made, after the first sampler class, was a Lone Star. Remember, I live in Texas. No one told me it was a difficult quilt to make. In fact, I was told it was a quilt that could be made quickly on the sewing machine. That was 1982, and the rotary cutter was available; but, the cutting mats had no lines, and the rulers were a set of plastic strips with no distinguishing marks on them whatsoever and were 1½"-wide, 2"-wide, 2½"-wide, and so forth.

As with any new technique, there are drawbacks. After making my first Lone Star, I ended up with a lot of leftover fabric. I remember making another Lone Star, taking the leftovers, rearranging the color sequence, and making a second quilt. That's a lot of "extra." As the saying goes, "we've come a long way."

The Star of Bethlehem was a popular pattern in both American and English patchwork in the late 1700s. In America, this design was given regional names, such as Star of the East, Rising Star, Rising Sun, Lone Star, Blazing Star, and Lone Star of Texas. British examples have been traced back as far as the late eighteenth century.

Most of the earlier star quilts were quite large. Several listed in the collection of the Shelburne Museum in Vermont are at least 110" x 110". Because of the exquisite fabrics and designs used in the early Star of Bethlehem quilts, many were likely made for special occasions.

As with any pattern, changes occur. The Broken Star is one such change. It first appeared sometime after the turn of the century. Many different color arrangements have developed from the basic pattern. Since we can make them so quickly, we can change the color arrangement and make a second quilt if the first one doesn't achieve the desired effect. A large print placed in just the right place makes a quilt come alive, sparkle. It's just wonderful how you can make this quilt pattern your own.

Experimenting with the 45°-angle cut opens up a world of quilts to be made. The quilts in this book are presented with the hope that they will inspire you to try your own hand at manipulating color and fabrics. The possibilities are limited only by your imagination.

GETTING STARTED

Rotary-cutting equipment is to the quilt world what the tire and wheel were to the automotive industry. Its invention was a revolution. How much easier quiltmaking has become! We no longer spend endless hours of marking and cutting with scissors. Not only is cutting with the rotary cutter much faster, it is much more accurate.

The quilts in this book were, at one time, considered very difficult to make. If you had told your grandmother you were going to make a Lone Star quilt, the response probably would have been something like, "Oh, that one is so hard for me!" or "You can't do that one, it's just too hard for an amateur quilter." Don't believe for even a moment that you can't make a Lone Star quilt, or any other "strip quilt" for that matter. All of the guesswork has been taken out of the quilting methods used today. The information in this book has been carefully thought out and presented in clear, step-by-step directions. You are told how many strips to cut and how wide to cut each one. Sewing directions are detailed enough for the beginning quilter. I find a Lone Star quilt easier and faster to make with fewer pitfalls than some block quilts that have many small pieces.

I have taught the Lone Star Quilt as a beginning class for eight years with excellent results. All that is required is cutting and sewing strips of fabric. It helps if the cutting and sewing are accurate; the more accurate, the better the quilt turns out. All of the other assembly tricks are carefully explained in detail.

The pride and joy within yourself when you show someone your finished quilt is beyond your wildest dreams. The oohs and ahs of "You did that all by yourself," or "Boy, I'm not that smart," you will hear over and over. We won't tell them how easy it is if you don't. You may want to share your newfound knowledge with a friend or relative. Otherwise, keep it a secret; we don't want the whole world to know how easy it is to make a Lone Star quilt!

FABRIC, TOOLS, AND SUPPLIES

As is the case with any project, the better your equipment, tools, and sewing supplies, the easier that project is to complete. The finished article will look better, too. What a shame to see a quilt that you know took a lot of time and effort, with batting bearding through the quilt top because a loose-weave fabric was used, just to save a few cents a yard. I'm not opposed to bargains, just be sure you are getting a true bargain.

I use 100% cotton fabric. It is easy to work with both in piecing and quilting. There are times when a particular color is needed that you might use a polyester blend. Just be aware that it can stretch and pull out of shape. The quilts in this book all have sides that are on the bias. As long as the fabrics are 100% cotton, I can still fit the pieces together.

When teaching classes on the Lone Star, the person in the class who is having trouble usually has a fabric of "undetermined" origin. To check a piece of fabric you are unsure of, cut off a small piece, lay it in a dish (not plastic), and light a match to it. After it has burned, if the ash is soft, it's 100% cotton. If there is a brittle, crisp substance left, then there was some polyester in the fabric.

All fabric should be prewashed before cutting. This allows the fabric to shrink and "bleed" before it's sewn into a quilt. If you prefer the finish of new fabric like I do, use a fabric finisher while pressing your fabric, after it has been washed.

When you purchase fabric for any of the patterns in this book, make a color-swatch card like the one shown. If your shop doesn't offer one, ask for a piece of paper and tape. Since yardage requirements for each fabric vary, you may not remember what fabric goes where when you get home. Having a swatch card in front of you as you sew will help eliminate some of those seams you inevitably have to "unsew."

All the quilts in this book are Template-Free®. This means they are all made by cutting strips of fabric, sewing the strips together, and then making a second cut, without using templates. This is all done with a rotary cutter, mat, and ruler. I use the large rotary cutter but have recently found the small one to have many good uses, too. I use a mat that is 17" x 23" with grid lines. These lines really help keep the strip sets straight when making the second cut. I use the Rotary Rule™ and Rotary Mate™ rulers designed by Trudie Hughes. I find them to be quite accurate, easy to use, and I can cut most anything with them.

All strips are cut on the cross grain of the fabric, with ¼"-wide seam allowances included. If the directions say to cut 2" strips, then cut 2" strips. They will finish to 1½". Yardage requirements provided for quilt patterns have a little to spare and are based on 40 usable

PROJECT

Fabric

A (1) ———————

B (2) ———————

C (3) ———————

D (4) ———————

E (5) ———————

F (6) ———————

G (7) ———————

H (8) ———————

I (9) ———————

J (10) ———————

inches after preshrinking. You may get an extra second cut if your fabric is wider.

Occasionally, I will use scissors. I keep a good, sharp 4" pair by my sewing machine. An ironing board at the correct height and a good iron are a necessity. Correct pressing makes everything go together easily.

I recently purchased a new sewing machine. I told the shop proprietor that all I wanted was a good straight stitch and a machine that didn't "eat" my little corners. I didn't feel like I needed the needle-up/needle-down option, but it came with the machine and what a joy! When your budget allows, treat yourself to a good sewing machine. It makes all the difference in the world.

If you have all the proper fabric, tools, and supplies, you are ready to make quilts. Let's begin.

> **Note:** You can use the star diagram on the title page of this book to plan color placement in your quilts. Place tracing paper over star diagram and color, or make several photocopies of it and play with the color placement.

GENERAL INSTRUCTIONS

Read the general instructions before you start a quilt. These instructions are presented up front so they don't have to be repeated with each set of quilt instructions.

Cutting Strips

Unless otherwise stated, all strips are cut across the fabric width (crosswise grain). The strips will be approximately 40" to 44" wide. Before cutting, make sure the selvages are even (parallel) and that there are no wrinkles along the folded edge of the fabric.

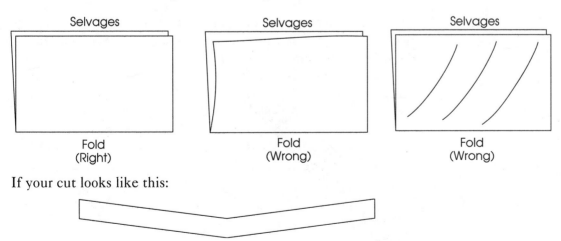

If your cut looks like this:

it means your fabric was not folded correctly. The slightest **V** can present a problem when sewing strips together. This is why I do not fold the fabric a second time. A second fold just gives you the opportunity to get a strip with three zigzags.

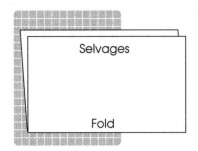

Lay the fabric on the cutting mat with the fold toward you, the raw edges to the left (reverse, if left-handed), and the selvages at the top of the mat.

Place the edge of a ruler inside the raw edge of the fabric. To make a cut at a right angle to the fold, lay one edge of another ruler along the fold of the fabric and adjust the straight ruler so that it is flush with the side of the second ruler on the fold.

Use the measurements on the ruler and mat to keep cuts straight. To cut an accurate 2"-wide strip, place the 2" line of the ruler on the edge of the fabric. You should not see any fabric to the left of the 2" line, and you should not see any of the mat between the fabric and the 2" line. Remember, if your strips are not cut accurately, there is no amount of sewing that will make your pieces fit.

All measurements given for cut strips include ¼"-wide seam allowances. Therefore, a strip cut 3" will finish to 2½".

Making Secondary Cuts

All the quilts in this book are made from diamonds. In traditional strip piecing, strips are assembled as shown at left.

The strips in this book are offset slightly, about the same amount as the width of the cut strip. Do not measure with a ruler; your estimate will be okay.

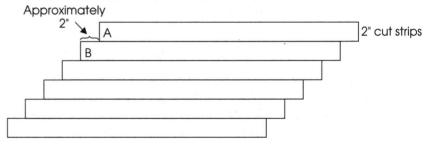

The second cut is made on a 45° angle. Don't panic; it's not that difficult. Place a 90° right triangle along one edge and a rotary ruler to the left of it as shown.

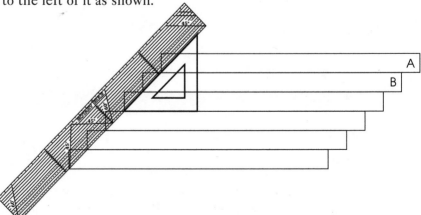

The 45°-angle line on the ruler should line up on a seam or on a line of the mat. I line them up on both. Move the right triangle out of the way and cut. Cut each strip unit in the dimensions specified for each quilt.

As you cut, check for accuracy with the right triangle, about every third cut. *This is extremely important!* Otherwise, the angles of the diamonds may vary and may be difficult to piece together accurately. Cut all strips from the strip unit and stack like units together.

Pressing

Pressing seams is probably the most neglected technique in quiltmaking. In speed piecing, the direction of the seam is decided as you go and not by where you will quilt, as it is in hand piecing. The direction a seam is pressed aids in assembly. It can also cause problems with the second cut if not pressed correctly.

Press from the right side, with the strips lying across the ironing board crosswise, not lengthwise. If you press lengthwise, you may get a curve.

Pressing from the right side of the strips prevents pleats or tucks, which can then make your strip set narrower than it should be. Press seams in the direction of the arrow as shown in the piecing diagrams.

It takes a little getting used to, but if you place the strip set across the ironing board, you can feel the seams and, with practice, become accustomed to this technique.

Assembling Diamonds

Place two of the second-cut strips with right sides together. Place a pin from the wrong side in the top strip, where the ¼" seam will cross the seam already made. Then place the pin into the right side of the second strip where the seams will cross, ¼" from the raw edge.

Repeat for each seam intersection. Seams must cross exactly ¼" from the raw edge. Pinch and hold the spot together with your thumb and index finger. Remove the pin and replace on either side of this spot. This way, there will be no distortion or movement of the fabric. If you make more than one quilt from this book, you may learn how to avoid pinning. It is possible!

As you pin the two strips together, there will be a small tip of the second strip showing at one end and a small tip of the first strip hanging over at the other end. Sew from the V formed at one end of the strip to the V formed at the other. If you do this carefully, the outside edge of the point will be a straight edge. If it is not, go back and make sure the seams begin and end at the point of the V. Restitch, if necessary.

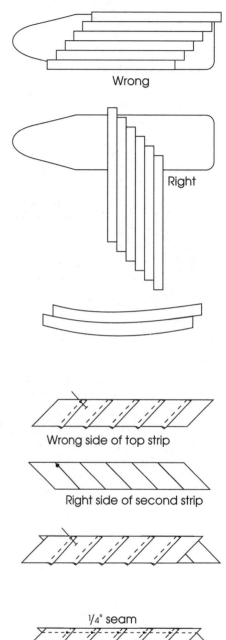

Wrong

Right

Wrong side of top strip

Right side of second strip

¼" seam

Press all seams for each diamond in one direction. Move the tip of your iron between the two strips and turn the iron to the side so the long edge of the iron presses the seam.

Sew three pairs of strips together to make one pieced diamond. Press all seams in the same direction. There should be no pleats or tucks.

Assembling Stars

Although the stars in this book are different sizes, the assembly is the same. Each star will have eight pieced diamonds (the star points), some made with only four small diamonds and some made with as many as thirty-six diamonds.

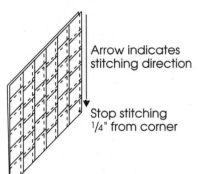

Arrow indicates stitching direction

Stop stitching ¼" from corner

Pin two pieced diamonds together, matching the seams between each diamond. Stitch from one end of the pieced diamond to within ¼" of the opposite end as shown. Backstitch to be sure this seam will not come loose when the corners or side triangles are inserted.

Leave the two sets of diamonds right sides together and press as described above in "Pressing" on page 9. Repeat with remaining diamonds.

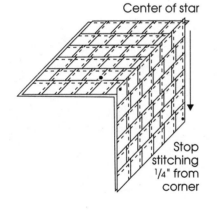

Center of star

Stop stitching ¼" from corner

Pin two sets of "twos" together to form half of the star, matching the seams between each diamond. Sew from one end to within ¼" of the opposite end as shown. Backstitch to secure the seam. Press seams between the pieced diamonds in the same direction.

Pin the star halves together, matching all seams between diamonds. If seams were pressed correctly, they will butt together and lie flat. Sew from one side of the star to the other. Press seams of the pieced diamonds on the reverse side of the star in the same direction.

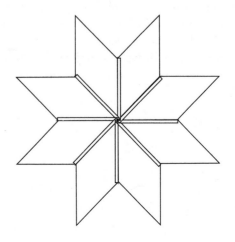

Measuring & Inserting Side Triangles & Corner Squares

After the star is assembled, half of the outside raw edges will be bias and the other half will not. It is necessary at this point to get an average measurement. The patterns give you the size that I cut. But since I know everyone doesn't make the same-size seams and there's a certain amount of stretch, everyone should measure their own. The larger the star, the more variance there can be. Measure ¼" from the inside corner to where the actual point will be.

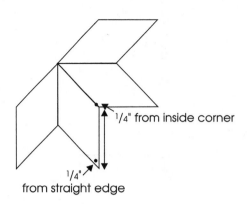

¼" from inside corner

¼" from straight edge

Measure all sixteen sides and list them on a piece of paper.

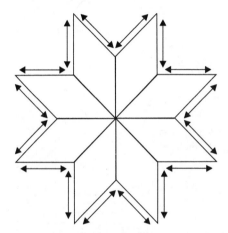

Take an average measurement. For example, if your measurements range from 20" to 22", the average will be 21". Let's hope you don't have that much variance. Accurate piecing should keep the shortest and longest measurements to within an inch.

For corner squares, add ½" seam allowances to the average measurement and cut 4 squares. Example: 21" + ½" = 21½"; cut 4 squares, each 21½" x 21½".

For the side triangles, multiply the average measurement (before the ½" was added) by 1.414, round up to the nearest ¼", and add 1¼" for seam allowances. Example: 21" x 1.414 = 29.69", rounded up to the next ¼" = 29.75" (29¾"), plus 1¼" for seam allowances, yields a final measurement of 31". Cut one square 31" x 31", then cut diagonally twice. The long side of each triangle will be on the outside edge of your quilt and have a straight edge. The other two sides are bias and make fitting the triangle into the quilt easier.

Cutting a large square, such as a 31" one, on the diagonal may be difficult if your ruler is not long enough. To make it easier, fold the square in half. Be sure the corners are even.

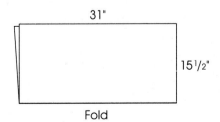

31"

15½"

Fold

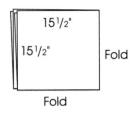

Fold

Fold

Then fold in half again to make a square. Be sure the corners are even!

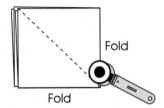

Fold

Fold

Cut *once* on the diagonal from the corner that has folds on both sides. You will have four side triangles.

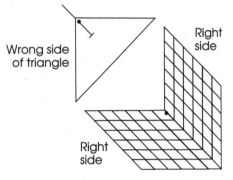

Insert side triangles first. From the wrong side of the fabric, place a pin in the corner of the triangle as shown, ¼" from the straight edges. Then place the pin into the right side of the pieced diamonds, ¼" from the inside corner. This should be the spot where you made a couple of backstitches when sewing the two pieced diamonds together. For ease in reading, only two diamond points are shown in the following illustrations.

Match the point of the triangle to the point of the pieced diamond. The points should meet exactly. Pin triangle in place. Sew from the outer edge to the inside corner pin. Sew as close to the corner pin as possible without sewing into it or past it.

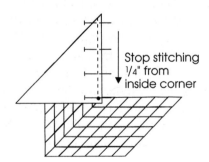

Stop stitching ¼" from inside corner

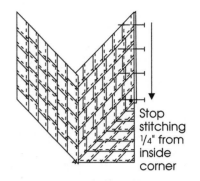

Rotate the other point of the background triangle to the point of the second pieced diamond. Remember, point to point. This time you will sew on the side with the diamonds. Sew from the outer edge to the inside corner. Do not sew into or past the backstitched spot. If necessary, stop a stitch short of the spot. This will keep you from sewing in unwanted pleats or tucks.

Stop stitching ¼" from inside corner

Repeat for the other three side triangles. *Press the seams toward the pieced diamonds.*

Insert the corner squares. With right sides together, place a pin in one corner of the square, ¼" from the edges, and into the inside corner of the pieced diamond. Pin a second corner of the square to the point of the pieced diamond on the left. There will be a small point of the pieced diamond protruding from the right edge, and the square will be even with the top edge of the side triangle. Sew from the outer edge to the inside corner. Do not go past the backstitched spot of the inside corner.

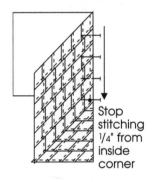

Stop stitching ¼" from inside corner

Pin a third corner of the square to the right-hand point of the pieced diamonds. There will be a small point of the pieced diamond protruding from the top edge. Sew from the outer edge to the inside corner, on the side with the pieced diamonds. Do not go past the backstitched spot of the inside corner. Press seams toward the pieced diamonds. Repeat for the other three corner squares.

Stop stitching ¼" from inside corner

Floating the Star

On large quilts, I like to float the star. A frame made from the background fabric emphasizes the points of the star. I usually add 1", but if you need to increase the size, it could be 2". For a 1"-wide finished frame, cut strips 1½" wide and piece to make long strips. Follow directions for "Straight-Cut Borders," pages 15, to attach the floating frame. This squares up the quilt. If you are adding a 2"-wide frame, cut strips 2½" wide.

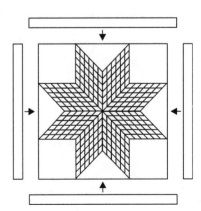

BORDERS

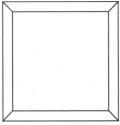 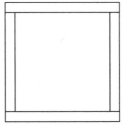

Mitered borders   Straight-cut borders

I do not like to add "busy" borders. I like stars and that's what I want to see. Each individual pattern will give border measurements as I made them. Feel free to improvise and add your own personal touch. Borders can be either mitered or straight cut. In either case, it's important to measure the finished quilt top carefully to calculate the required length for the border strips.

Mitered Borders

For perfectly flat mitered corners, follow the directions below as shown for the sample quilt top, substituting your quilt measurements in the formula. The key is accurate measuring and cutting.

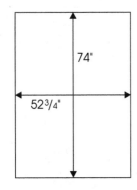

1. Measure and record the length and width of the quilt at the centers, from raw edge to raw edge. For the sample quilt at left, the width is 52¾" and the length is 74".

2. Decide on the total finished width of the border(s). I've used a 7" finished width in the example. Add two finished border widths to the measurement determined above.

$$
\begin{array}{ll}
52\tfrac{3}{4}" & 74" \\
+14" & +14" \\
\hline
66\tfrac{3}{4}" & 88"
\end{array}
$$

The measurement of the top in the example, from raw edge to raw edge after borders are added, will be 66¾" x 88". Cut the border strips ¼" wider than the desired finished width, in this case 7¼". Cut two strips, each 7¼" x 66¾" (the determined finished width), and two strips, each 7¼" x 88" (the determined finished length). Be sure these are cut exactly to length.

Note: If you cut the border strips across the fabric width (crosswise grain), it will be necessary to piece the border strips to the correct length(s).

3. At each end of each border strip, measure in and mark the desired finished border width, plus ¼". Mark the center of each border strip.

7¼"   Center   7¼"

4. Mark the ¼" seam intersection on all four corners of the quilt top. Mark the center of each side of the quilt top.

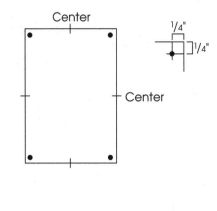

Center

Center

5. Attach all four borders, matching centers and the marks at the end of the border strips to the corner marks on the quilt top. Stitch, easing the quilt onto the border, if necessary. Begin and end stitching exactly at the corner marks, backstitching a few stitches to secure.

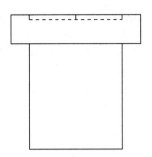

6. With right sides together, fold quilt diagonally so border strips match at one corner. Check to see that the outside corner is square and that there is no extra fullness at the edges. Using a marking pen and a ruler, draw a straight line from the outer corner of the binding to the mark on the border at the quilt corner. Stitch on the line, ending a half stitch from the mark at the inner corner. Backstitch. Trim away excess border, leaving ¼" seam allowance.

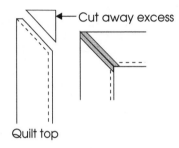

Cut away excess

Quilt top

7. Repeat with remaining corners. Press seams open.

Straight-Cut Borders

1. Measure the length of the quilt top at the center, from raw edge to raw edge. Cut two border strips to that measurement in the desired width, plus ½" for seam allowances.

   Note: If you cut the border strips across the fabric width (crosswise grain), it will be necessary to piece the borders to the correct lengths.

   Mark the center of each side of the quilt and the center of each border strip.

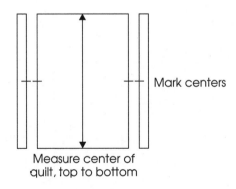

Mark centers

Measure center of quilt, top to bottom

2. Join border strips to the sides of the quilt with a ¼"-wide seam allowance, matching the ends and centers and easing the quilt to the border as needed. Press seams toward the border.

3. Measure the width of the quilt at the center, from raw edge to raw edge, including the two borders that you just added. Cut two border strips to that measurement in the desired width, plus ½" for seam allowances. Mark the center of the top and bottom of the quilt and the center of each border strip.

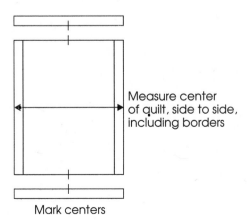

Measure center of quilt, side to side, including borders

Mark centers

Join the strips to the top and bottom of the quilt, matching centers and easing the quilt onto the border strip as necessary. Press seams toward the border.

PREPARING TO QUILT

It's easier to mark the quilt top before layering it with the batting and backing. Choose a marking tool in a color that will be visible on the fabric. For some quilts, you will need more than one color. For light-colored fabrics, a mechanical or hard lead pencil is often best. Water-soluble pens are also available, but, in my experience, it is sometimes difficult to remove the marks from solid-colored fabrics. You can also use ¼"-wide masking tape as a stitching guide. I recommend positioning it as needed, rather than applying it to the entire quilt top, since it may be difficult to remove and often leaves a sticky residue on the surface of your quilt if left in place too long.

To mark dark-colored fabrics, I use a pink or yellow marking pencil, available at your local quilt shop. Both of these show up nicely on nearly all dark fabrics. Whatever you choose for marking, test it first on scraps of the fabric from your quilt to make sure you can remove it easily.

Once the quilting design is marked, layer the quilt with batting and backing and baste the layers together.

1. Place the backing, wrong side up, on a flat surface and smooth it out to remove any wrinkles. Then tape it in place or pin it to the carpet on the floor.
2. Spread the batting of your choice on top of the backing, then add the quilt top, smoothing out any wrinkles and pinning through all layers down and across the center of the quilt. Use long straight pins if you are basting for hand quilting.

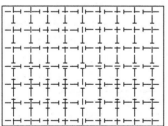

3. Continue pinning, placing pins 3" to 4" apart. Using a long darning needle, baste the layers together in a grid, spacing the rows of basting 4" to 6" apart. The more you baste, the less likely the quilt layers will shift while you work.

4. Remove the pins and you are ready to quilt. If you prefer, you can pin-baste the layers together for machine quilting, using safety pins spaced a hand's width apart across the surface of the quilt. The thicker the batting, the closer the pins should be.

The quilting on a quilt is like the icing on a cake. I recommend taking a good class to learn the proper techniques for making the tiny hand stitches every quilter and quilt enthusiast covets.

BINDING

To finish the raw edges of your quilt, you will need to make your own binding. Binding can be cut on the straight grain or on the bias. Straight-grain binding requires less fabric, and some quilters say it prevents the outside edge of the quilt from rippling. But because it is cut on the straight grain, there will be a single thread that runs the length of the quilt along the outer edge; it will get more wear than the remaining threads in the binding. That means, the edge could wear out sooner. For that reason, I prefer binding that has been cut on the bias.

I also prefer doubled binding for its added strength and durability. For doubled binding, I cut bias strips 2½" wide for a finished width of ⅜".

To make enough doubled bias binding for a wall or crib quilt, you will need ½ yard of fabric. For a twin-size, buy ¾ yard. One yard is adequate for either a full- or queen-size quilt, and you'll need 1¼ yards for binding a king-size quilt.

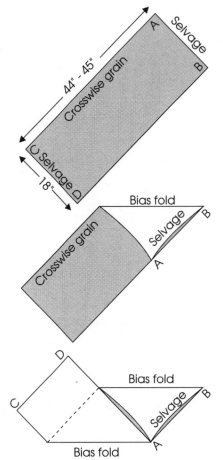

To make doubled bias binding:
1. Fold a square of fabric on the bias.

OR
Fold a ½-yard piece for quick cutting bias strips, following the illustrations at right and paying careful attention to the location of the lettered corners.

2. Cut strips 2½" wide, cutting perpendicular to the folds as shown.

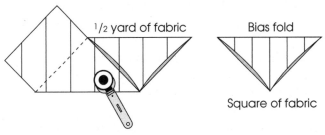

3. Sew strips, right sides together, to make one long piece of binding. Press seams open.

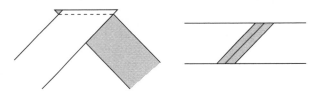

Fold

4. Fold strip in half, wrong sides together, and press.

To attach binding to the quilt:

1. Unfold binding at one end and turn under ¼" at a 45° angle as shown, so you start sewing with a finished edge at the end of the binding. Turning it under at an angle distributes the bulk where the two ends will come together.

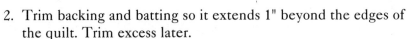

Fold line

2. Trim backing and batting so it extends 1" beyond the edges of the quilt. Trim excess later.

3. Starting on one side of the quilt, stitch the binding to the quilt with the raw edges of the binding even with the raw edges of the quilt top. (Backing and batting will extend beyond the edge.) Stitch ⅜" from raw edges. End stitching ⅜" from corner. Backstitch. Remove from sewing machine.

4. To miter corner, fold binding up, away from the quilt.

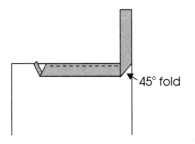
45° fold

5. Fold binding back down onto itself, parallel with the edge of the quilt. A fold will form in the binding, parallel with the raw edge of the quilt at the upper corner. Start stitching at the edge, ending stitching ⅜" from the next corner. Repeat the mitering steps at each corner.

Fold

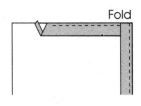

6. When you reach the beginning of the binding, cut bias 1" longer than needed and tuck the end inside the beginning of the strip.

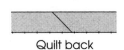
Quilt back

7. Trim away excess batting and backing. Fold the binding over the raw edges of the quilt and blindstitch in place, with the folded edge covering the row of machine stitching.

At each corner, a miter will form. Hand stitch miters in place.

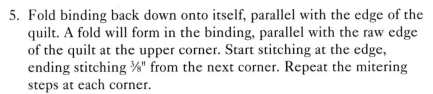
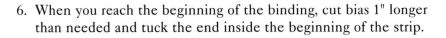
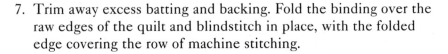
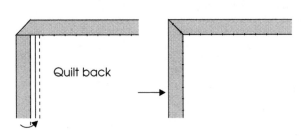
Quilt back

QUILT PATTERNS

Pennsylvania Star

Color photos:
pages 28 and 29

Quilt size:
91" x 91"

Materials: 44"-wide fabric

Fabric A: 7 yds.
(Stars, background, and borders)

Fabric B: 2 yds.
(Stars)

Binding: 1 yd.
Backing: 7¾ yds.

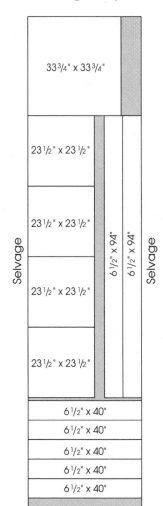

Cutting

All strips are cut across fabric width (crosswise grain), unless otherwise specified.

Fabric A:
Star Strips
23 strips, each 2½" x 40"
4 strips, each 4½" x 40"

Borders
Cut borders before cutting side triangles and corner squares, following the cutting layout.
5 strips, each 6½" x 40", for pieced side borders
2 strips, each 6½" x 94", for top and bottom borders

Corner Squares and Triangles

Note: To be on the safe side, you may want to wait until star is assembled to measure and cut corner squares and side triangles.

4 squares, each 23½" x 23½", for corner squares
1 square, 33¾" x 33¾". Cut twice diagonally to make 4 side setting triangles. See page 12 for cutting a large square.

Fabric B:
23 strips, each 2½" x 40"

Directions

Unit 1
Make 15

Unit 2
Make 8

Star Points

1. Sew 2½" strips together to create the number of each unit shown in the piecing diagram at left. Letters indicate the color placement. Offset the strips about 2½". Press seams in the direction of the arrows from the right side of the fabric so no pleats or tucks are pressed in.

2. Refer to the directions, "Making Secondary Cuts," pages 8–9, to make the following units.

   Place Unit 1 and Unit 2 with right sides together on the cutting mat. Make 2 cuts, each 8½" wide. I use a 6"-wide ruler, plus 2½" from another ruler, or a 12" square. Separate the 8½" diamonds into 2 stacks, Unit 3 and Unit 4. Make 2 more cuts, each 2½" wide, and separate into 2 stacks.

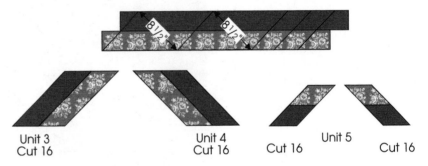

Unit 3
Cut 16

Unit 4
Cut 16

Unit 5
Cut 16

Cut 16

Repeat 7 more times with Unit 1 and Unit 2 strips placed right sides together.

Using the 4½" strips of Fabric A, make a secondary cut. Open the strips, stack, and cut all 4 strips at once into 4½"-wide strips. Cut 16 diamonds.

Unit 6
Make 16

3. Sew 2 of Unit 5 together to make Unit 6 as shown.

4. Cut the remaining Unit 1 strips with right sides facing up into 2½"-wide strips. Sew 2 strips together to make Unit 7 as shown.

Unit 7
Make 32

5. Sew a 4½" diamond to Unit 7 as shown.

Make 16

6. Sew together 2 of the units assembled in step 5 as shown.

Make 8

7. Sew one Unit 3 to the left side of the unit made in step 6. Sew a second Unit 3 to the right side as shown.

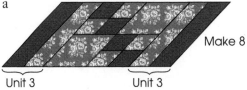

Make 8

Unit 3   Unit 3

8. Sew Unit 6 and Unit 7 to Unit 4 as shown.

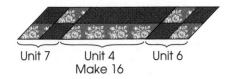

Unit 7   Unit 4   Unit 6

Make 16

9. Sew unit assembled in step 8 to one side of the unit assembled in step 7.

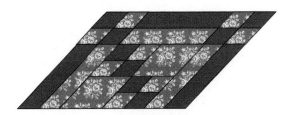

10. Rotate unit assembled in step 8 and sew to opposite side.

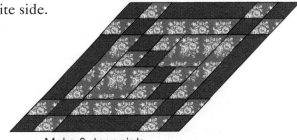

Make 8 star points

Quilt Top Assembly

Refer to pages 10–13, "Assembling Stars" and "Measuring and Inserting Side Triangles and Corner Squares."

1. Assemble pieced diamonds in sets of two. Join 2 sets of "twos" to form half of the star. Then join the completed star halves together in a straight seam from one side of the star to the other.
2. Measure for corner squares and side triangles.
3. Insert side triangles, then corner squares.
4. Add border. (See pages 14–15.)

Finishing

1. Mark top for quilting.
2. Layer with batting and backing; quilt.
3. Bind edges with bias strips of fabric.

Children's Pinwheel

Color photo:
page 38

Quilt size:
66" x 66"

Materials: 44"-wide fabric
See color key below
Fabric A: ⁵⁄₈ yd.
Fabric B: 1³⁄₈ yds.
Fabric C: ⁵⁄₈ yd.
Background: 1¾ yds.
Outer border & binding: 1⁷⁄₈ yds.
Backing: 4 yds.

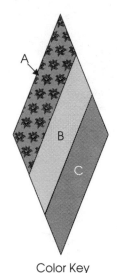

Color Key

Cutting

All strips are cut across fabric width (crosswise grain), unless otherwise specified.

Fabrics A, B, and C:
7 strips, each 2¼" wide, from each fabric for a total of 21 strips

Background fabric:
4 strips, each 8" x 40". Crosscut to make 16 corner squares, each 8" x 8".
2 strips, each 11¾" x 40". Crosscut to make 4 squares, each 11¾" x 11¾". Cut twice diagonally to make 8 side triangles.

Fabric B:
9 strips, each 2" x 40", for sashing and inner border

Outer border fabric:
4 strips, each 5½" wide, cut on the lengthwise grain of the fabric. Wait until blocks are assembled to cut borders to required lengths.

Directions

Star Points

1. Sew the 2¼"-wide strips together to make 7 of the units shown at right. Letters indicate the color placement. Offset the strips about 2¼". Press seams in the direction of the arrow.

Make 7

2. Using a 6"-wide ruler, follow directions, "Making Secondary Cuts," pages 8–9, to make the following units. Cut strips 5¾" wide.

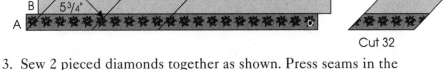

Cut 32

3. Sew 2 pieced diamonds together as shown. Press seams in the direction of the arrow.

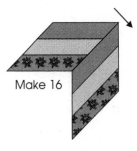

Make 16

Quilt Top Assembly

Refer to pages 10–13, "Assembling Stars" and "Measuring and Inserting Side Triangles and Corner Squares."

1. Continue star assembly. This star has fewer seams than most, so the corner squares and side triangles fit easily. Make 4 stars.
2. Cut 2 sashing strips, each 25½" long, from the 2"-wide sashing strips cut earlier. Measure Star blocks to be sure this is the correct length. Add sashing between blocks.

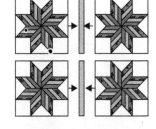

3. Piece the remaining 7 sashing and inner border strips together at the 2" ends to make one long strip. Cut 1 strip 52" long. (Double-check the measurement of your blocks before cutting this strip.) Join 2 rows of blocks with the 52"-long sashing strip.
4. Add straight-cut inner borders. (See page 15.)
5. Add outer borders, mitering corners. (See pages 14–15.)

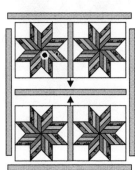

Finishing

1. Mark top for quilting.
2. Layer with batting and backing; quilt.
3. Bind edges with bias strips of fabric.

Lone Star with a Ninepatch

Color photos:
page 33

Quilt size:
84" x 84"

Materials: 44"-wide fabric
See color key below
Fabric A: 1¼ yds.
Fabric B: 1½ yds.
Fabric C: 1 yd.
Background: 2¾ yds.
Inner border: ½ yd.

Outer border: 1¾ yds.
(cut crosswise)
OR
2½ yds. (cut lengthwise)

Binding: 1 yd.
Backing: 5¼ yds.

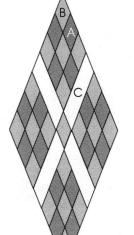

Color Key

Cutting

All strips are cut across fabric width (crosswise grain).

From the following fabrics, cut the number of strips given in the widths indicated.

	Number of Strips
Fabric A – 2½"	15
Fabric B – 2½"	18
Fabric C – 6½"	4

Background fabric:

Note: To be on the safe side, you may want to wait until star is assembled to measure and cut corner squares and side triangles.

4 squares, each 20¾" x 20¾", for corner squares

1 square, 29¾" x 29¾". Cut twice diagonally to make 4 side setting triangles.

Inner border fabric:
8 strips, each 1½" x 40", to float star

Outer border fabric:
8 strips, each 6½" x 40"

Note: If you prefer unpieced borders, fold the yardage crosswise until the piece measures 22" x 45". Cut away selvage along one edge. Then cut 4 strips, each 6½" wide, for 4 unpieced border strips.

Directions

Star Points

1. Sew strips together to create the number of each unit shown in the piecing diagram at right. Letters indicate the color placement. Offset the strips about 2½". Press seams in the direction of the arrows from the right side of the fabric so no pleats or tucks are pressed in.

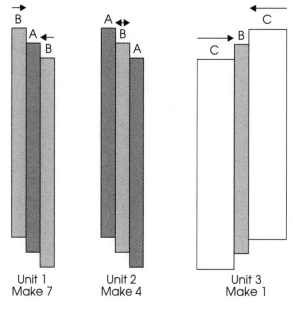

Unit 1
Make 7

Unit 2
Make 4

Unit 3
Make 1

2. Follow directions, "Making Secondary Cuts," pages 8–9, to make the following units.

From Unit 1, cut 64 strips, each 2½" wide.

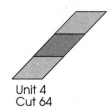

Unit 4
Cut 64

From Unit 2, cut 32 strips, each 2½" wide.

Unit 5
Cut 32

From 2 strips of Fabric C, 6½" wide, opened to the full width, cut 16 strips, each 2½" wide.

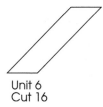

Unit 6
Cut 16

From Unit 3, cut 8 strips, each 2½" wide. Notice that the 45° angle faces the other way.

2½"

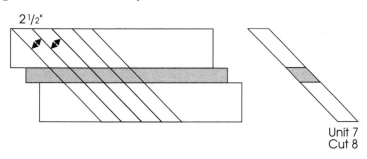

Unit 7
Cut 8

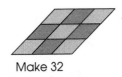

Make 32

3. Sew 2 of Unit 4 to 1 of Unit 5 to make a Ninepatch diamond as shown.

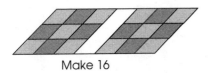

Make 16

4. Sew 1 Unit 6 between 2 Ninepatch diamonds.

5. Sew Unit 7 between 2 Ninepatch diamond units as shown.

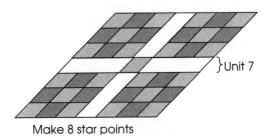

}Unit 7

Make 8 star points

Quilt Top Assembly

Refer to pages 10–13, "Assembling Stars" and "Measuring and Inserting Side Triangles and Corner Squares."

1. Assemble pieced diamonds in sets of two. Join 2 sets of "twos" to form half of the star. Then join the completed star halves together in a straight seam from one side of the star to the other.
2. Measure for corner squares and side triangles.
3. Insert side triangles, then corner squares.
4. Attach the 1½" frame of background fabric to float the star.(See page 13.)
5. Add outer borders, mitering corners. (See pages 14–15.)

Finishing

1. Mark top for quilting.
2. Layer with batting and backing; quilt.
3. Bind edges with bias strips of fabric.

GALLERY

Broken Star by Jo Parrott, 1992, Dallas, Texas, 103" x 103". This pattern is a long-time favorite of the author. Using Template-Free® techniques, she pieced this top in only about fourteen hours. Quilted by Mary Ray.

Pennsylvania Star by Jo Parrott, 1992, Dallas, Texas, 91" x 91". The quilt was the author's first in this series of Template-Free stars. It was so much fun, she immediately set up a class to teach her speed-piecing methods. Quilted by Audrey Couvillon.

Pennsylvania Star by Jo Parrott, 1992, Dallas, Texas, 67" x 67". Using a lighter floral background sets off this Pennslyvania Star. Quilted by Jo Parrott.

Radiating Lone Star by Mary Jane Brooks, 1992, Garland, Texas, 86" x 86". The bright blue in the star points is repeated in the border. Quilted by Jo Parrott.

Lone Star Flower by Jo Parrott, 1992, Dallas, Texas, 60" x 60". This fun, small quilt is excellent as a baby quilt. Quilted by Jo Parrott.

Lone Star Hopscotch by Jo Parrott, 1992, Dallas, Texas, 86" x 86". This quilt shows how you can place color wherever you want. Quilted by Audrey Couvillon.

Lone Star Reverse Repeat by Jo Parrott, 1992, Dallas, Texas, 86" x 86". Receiving the large print fabric in the shop one day, Jo made this quilt the next day. Quilted by Audrey Couvillon.

Lone Star with a Ninepatch (light) by Jo Parrott, 1992, Dallas, Texas, 84" x 84". A dark outer border sets off this pastel star. Quilted by Jo Parrott.

Lone Star with a Ninepatch (dark) by Anita Kienker, 1992, Rockwall, Texas, 84" x 84". An inner border of the background fabric helps "float" the star. Quilted by Jo Parrott.

Polaris Star by Jo Parrott, 1992, Dallas, Texas, 79" x 100". This scrap quilt was quilted by the author's daughter-in-law, Dana Parrott, and claimed by her grandson Casey.

Alabama Star by Jo Parrott, 1992, Dallas, Texas, 102" x 102". The bright, large, red print was the inspiration for this quilt. Quilted by Mary Ray.

Carpenter's Wheel by Jo Parrott, 1992, Dallas, Texas, 84" x 84". Using her speed-piecing techniques, Jo put this quilt top together in a lot less time than it took for its antique counterpart. Quilted by Jo Parrott.

1,000 Pyramids (light) by Jo Parrott, 1992, Dallas, Texas, 84" x 90". Looking at a picture of a 1,000 Pyramids quilt, Jo decided diamonds could take on the look of triangles. And they do! Quilted by Mary Ray.

1,000 Pyramids (dark) by Anita Kienker, 1992, Rockwall, Texas, 66" x 90". This darker version gives a completely different look to the pattern. Quilted by Jo Parrott.

Children's Pinwheel by Jo Parrott, 1992, Dallas, Texas, 66" x 66". This bright, colorful quilt is perfect for a child. Quilted by Jo Parrott.

Lone Star Flower

Color photo:
page 31

Quilt size:
60" x 60"

Materials: 44"-wide fabric
See color key below

Fabric A: 1 yd.
Fabric B: ½ yd.
Fabric C: ½ yd.
Fabric D: ⅛ yd.
Fabric E: ½ yd.
Background: 1¾ yds.

Border: 1 yd.
(cut crosswise)
OR
1¾ yds. (cut lengthwise)

Binding: ¾ yd.
Backing: 3¾ yds.

Cutting

All strips are cut across fabric width (crosswise grain).

From the following fabrics, cut the number of strips given in the widths indicated.

	Number of Strips
Fabric A – 6½"	2
– 2½"	4
Fabric B – 2½"	4
Fabric C – 2½"	4
Fabric D – 2½"	1
Fabric E – 2½"	4

Background fabric:

Note: To be on the safe side, you may want to wait until star is assembled to measure and cut corner squares and side triangles.

2 strips, each 14¾" x 40". Cross-cut to make 4 corner squares, each 14¾" x 14¾".
1 square 21½" x 21½". Cut twice diagonally to make 4 side triangles.

Border fabric:
6 strips, each 4½" wide, cut crosswise and pieced to required lengths;
OR
4 strips, each 4½" wide, cut on the lengthwise grain for unpieced borders.

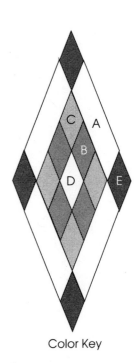

Color Key

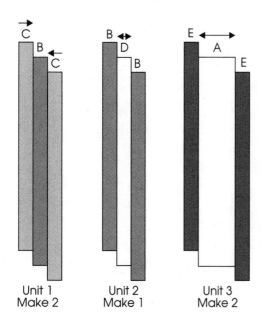

Unit 1
Make 2

Unit 2
Make 1

Unit 3
Make 2

Directions

Star Points

1. Sew strips together to create the number of each unit indicated in the piecing diagram, left. Letters indicate the color placement. Offset the strips about 2½". Press seams in the direction of the arrows.

2. Follow directions, "Making Secondary Cuts," pages 8–9, to make the following units.

   From Unit 1, cut 16 strips, each 2½" wide.

Unit 4
Cut 16

From Unit 2, cut 8 strips, each 2½" wide.

Unit 5
Cut 8

Using the 2½"-wide strips from Fabric A opened to their full width, cut 16 strips, each 6½" wide. Do not leave fabric doubled; otherwise you will get a reverse cut for half of the strips.

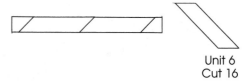

Unit 6
Cut 16

From Unit 3, cut 16 strips, each 2½" wide.

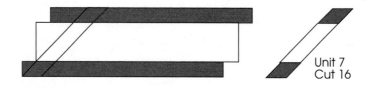

Unit 7
Cut 16

3. Sew 2 of Unit 4 and 1 of Unit 5 to make the flower units.

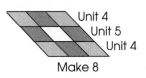

4. Sew Unit 6 to top and bottom of each flower unit. Then sew Unit 7 to each side as shown.

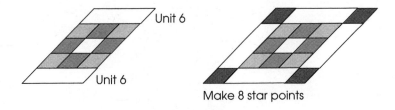

Make 8 star points

Quilt Top Assembly

Refer to pages 10–13, "Assembling Stars" and "Measuring and Inserting Side Triangles and Corner Squares."

1. Assemble pieced diamonds in sets of two. Join 2 sets of "twos" to form half of the star. Then join the completed star halves together in a straight seam from one side of the star to the other.
2. Measure for corner squares and side triangles.
3. Insert side triangles, then corner squares.
4. Add borders. (See pages 14–15.)

Finishing

1. Mark top for quilting.
2. Layer with batting and backing; quilt.
3. Bind edges with bias strips of fabric.

Lone Star Reverse Repeat

Color photo:
page 32

Quilt size:
86" x 86"

Materials: 44"-wide fabric
See color key below

Fabric A: ⅓ yd.
Fabric B: ½ yd.
Fabric C: ¾ yd.
Fabric D: ⅞ yd.
Fabric E: 1 yd.
Fabric F: ¾ yd.
Background: 3½ yds.

Border: 1½ yds.
(cut crosswise)
OR
2½ yds. (cut lengthwise)

Binding: 1 yd.
Backing: 5 yds.

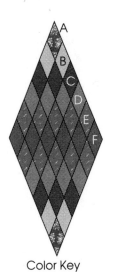

Color Key

Cutting

All strips are cut across fabric width (crosswise grain).

From the following fabrics, cut the number of 3"-wide strips indicated. For a wall hanging or crib quilt, cut strips only 2" wide.

	Number of Strips
Fabric A	2
Fabric B	4
Fabric C	6
Fabric D	8
Fabric E	10
Fabric F	6

Background fabric:

Note: To be on the safe side, you may want to wait until star is assembled to measure and cut corner squares and side triangles.

4 corner squares, each 22" x 22". Some fabrics are wide enough to enable you to cut 2 squares across the width of the fabric. Yardage requirements are based on fabrics that are *not* wide enough to do so.

1 square, 31¾" x 31¾". Cut twice diagonally to make 4 side triangles.

Border fabric:

9 strips, each 6½" wide, cut on the crosswise grain and pieced to required lengths
OR
4 strips, each 6½" wide, cut on the lengthwise grain for unpieced borders.

Directions

Star Points

1. Sew strips together to create the number of each unit shown in the piecing diagram at right. Letters indicate the color placement. Offset the strips about 3". Press seams in the direction of the arrows from the right side of the fabric so no pleats or tucks are pressed in.
2. Follow directions, "Making Secondary Cuts," pages 8–9, to make the following units.

    Cut strips 3" wide.

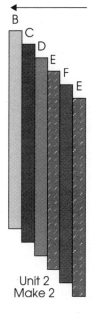

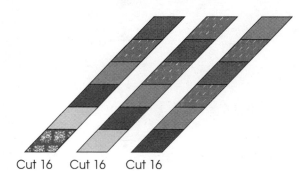

Cut 16   Cut 16   Cut 16

Unit 1
Make 2

Unit 2
Make 2

Unit 3
Make 3

3. Assemble 8 star points as shown.

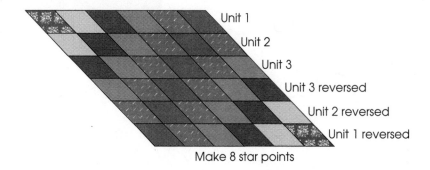

Unit 1
Unit 2
Unit 3
Unit 3 reversed
Unit 2 reversed
Unit 1 reversed

Make 8 star points

Quilt Top Assembly

Refer to pages 10–13, "Assembling Stars" and "Measuring and Inserting Side Triangles and Corner Squares."

1. Assemble pieced diamonds in sets of two. Join 2 sets of "twos" to form half of the star. Then join the completed star halves together in a straight seam from one side of the star to the other.
2. Measure for corner squares and side triangles.
3. Insert side triangles, then corner squares.
4. Add borders. (See pages 14–15.)

Finishing

1. Mark top for quilting.
2. Layer with batting and backing; quilt.
3. Bind edges with bias strips of fabric.

Radiating Lone Star

Color photo:
page 30

Quilt size:
86" x 86"

Materials: 44"-wide fabric
See color key below

Fabric A: ⅛ yd.
Fabric B: ¼ yd.
Fabric C: ⅓ yd.
Fabric D: ⅜ yd.
Fabric E: ½ yd.
Fabric F: ⅝ yd.
Fabric G: ½ yd.
Fabric H: ⅜ yd.
Fabric I: ⅓ yd.
Fabric J: ¼ yd.
Fabric K: ⅛ yd.
Background: 3½ yds.

Border: 1½ yds.
(cut crosswise)
OR
2½ yds. (cut lengthwise)

Binding: 1 yd.
Backing: 5¼ yds.

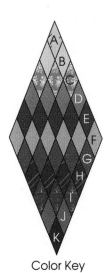

Color Key

Cutting

All strips are cut across fabric width (crosswise grain).

From the following fabrics, cut the number of 3"-wide strips indicated.

	Number of Strips
Fabric A	1
Fabric B	2
Fabric C	3
Fabric D	4
Fabric E	5
Fabric F	6
Fabric G	5
Fabric H	4
Fabric I	3
Fabric J	2
Fabric K	1

Background fabric:

Note: To be on the safe side, you may want to wait until star is assembled to measure and cut corner squares and side triangles.

- 4 corner squares, each 22" x 22". Some fabrics are wide enough to enable you to cut 2 squares across the width of the fabric. Yardage requirements are based on fabrics that are *not* wide enough to do so.
- 1 square, 31¾" x 31¾". Cut twice diagonally for 4 side triangles.

Border fabric:

9 strips, each 6½" wide, cut on the crosswise grain and pieced to required lengths
OR
4 strips, each 6½" wide, cut on the lengthwise grain for unpieced borders.

Directions

Star Points

1. Sew strips together to make 1 each of the units shown in the piecing diagram below. Letters indicate the color placement. Offset the strips about 3". Press seams in the direction of the arrows.

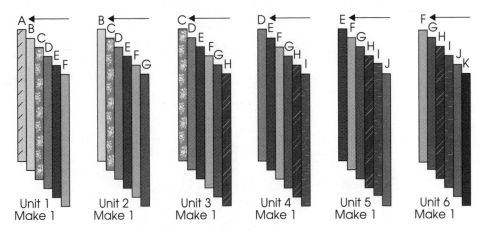

Unit 1
Make 1

Unit 2
Make 1

Unit 3
Make 1

Unit 4
Make 1

Unit 5
Make 1

Unit 6
Make 1

2. Follow directions, "Making Secondary Cuts," pages 8–9, to cut each of the units made above into 3"-wide strips. To keep each unit separate, pin a label to each set. Cut 8 strips from each unit.
3. Refer to "Assembling Diamonds," pages 9–10, and as shown at right to assemble 8 star points.

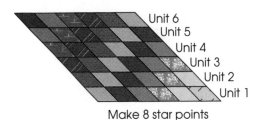

Make 8 star points

Quilt Top Assembly

Refer to pages 10–13, "Assembling Stars" and "Measuring and Inserting Side Triangles and Corner Squares."

1. Assemble pieced diamonds in sets of two. Join 2 sets of "twos" to form half of the star. Then join the completed star halves together in a straight seam from one side of the star to the other.
2. Measure for corner squares and side triangles.
3. Insert side triangles, then corner squares.
4. Add borders. (See pages 14–15.)

Finishing

1. Mark top for quilting.
2. Layer with batting and backing; quilt.
3. Bind edges with bias strips of fabric.

Lone Star Hopscotch

Color photo:

page 32

Quilt size:

86" x 86"

This Lone Star was designed to show you how to put a color ANYWHERE! Use the diagram in step 3 under Directions to help with color placement.

Materials: 44"-wide fabric

See color key below

Fabric A: ⅓ yd.
Fabric B: ⅜ yd.
Fabric C: ⅝ yd.
Fabric D: ⅜ yd.
Fabric E: ⅝ yd.
Fabric F: ⅜ yd.
Fabric G: ⅓ yd.
Fabric H: ⅜ yd.
Fabric I: ⅜ yd.
Background: 3½ yds.

Border: 1½ yds.
(cut crosswise)
OR
2½ yds. (cut lengthwise)

Binding: 1 yd.
Backing: 5¼ yds.

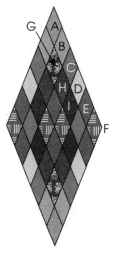

Color Key

Cutting

All strips are cut across fabric width (crosswise grain).

From the following fabrics, cut the number of 3"-wide strips indicated.

	Number of Strips
Fabric A	2
Fabric B	4
Fabric C	6
Fabric D	4
Fabric E	6
Fabric F	4
Fabric G	2
Fabric H	4
Fabric I	4

Background fabric:

Note: To be on the safe side, you may want to wait until star is as-sembled to measure and cut corner squares and side triangles.

4 corner squares, each 22" x 22". Some fabrics are wide enough to enable you to cut 2 squares across the width of the fabric. Yardage require-ments are based on fabrics that are *not* wide enough to do so.

1 square 31¾" x 31¾". Cut twice diagonally for 4 side triangles.

Border fabric:

9 strips, each 5½" wide, cut on the crosswise grain and pieced to required lengths
OR
4 strips, each 5½" wide, cut on the lengthwise grain for unpieced borders.

Directions

Star Points

1. Sew strips together to make 2 each of the units shown in the piecing diagram below. Letters indicate the color placement. Offset the strips about 3". Press seams in the direction of the arrows.

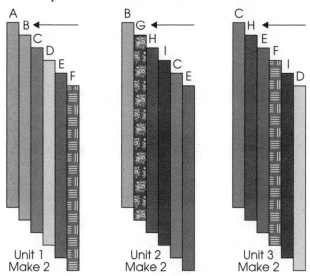

Unit 1
Make 2

Unit 2
Make 2

Unit 3
Make 2

2. Follow directions, "Making Secondary Cuts," pages 8–9, to cut each of the units made above into 3"-wide strips. To help keep each unit separate, pin a label to each set. Cut 16 strips from each unit.

3. Refer to "Assembling Diamonds," pages 9–10, and the diagram at right to assemble 8 star points.

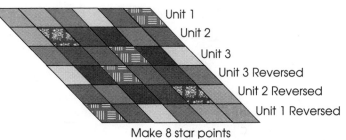

Unit 1
Unit 2
Unit 3
Unit 3 Reversed
Unit 2 Reversed
Unit 1 Reversed

Make 8 star points

Quilt Top Assembly

Refer to pages 10–13, "Assembling Stars" and "Measuring and Inserting Side Triangles and Corner Squares."

1. Assemble pieced diamonds in sets of two. Join 2 sets of "twos" to form half of the star. Then join the completed star halves together in a straight seam from one side of the star to the other.
2. Measure for corner squares and side triangles.
3. Insert side triangles, then corner squares.
4. Add borders. (See pages 14–15.)

Finishing

1. Mark top for quilting.
2. Layer with batting and backing; quilt.
3. Bind edges with bias strips of fabric.

Broken Star

Color photo:
page 27

Quilt size:
103" x 103"

Materials: 44"-wide fabric
See color key below

Fabric A: ½ yd.
Fabric B: 1 yd.
Fabric C: 1¼ yds.
Fabric D: 1½ yds.
Fabric E: 1¼ yds.
Fabric F: 1 yd.
Fabric G: ½ yd.
Background: 3¾ yds.

Border: 2¾ yds.
(cut crosswise)
OR
3 yds. (cut lengthwise)

Binding: 1¼ yds.
Backing: 9½ yds.

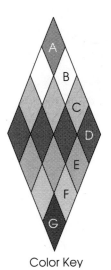

Color Key

Cutting

All strips are cut across fabric width (crosswise grain).

From the following fabrics, cut the number of 2¾"-wide strips indicated.

	Number of Strips
Fabric A	4
Fabric B	8
Fabric C	12
Fabric D	16
Fabric E	12
Fabric F	8
Fabric G	4

Background fabric:

Note: To be on the safe side, you may want to wait until star is assembled to measure and cut corner squares and side triangles.

12 background squares, each 13¼" x 13¼"

4 corner rectangles, each 13¼" x 26"

2 squares, each 19¼" x 19¼". Cut twice diagonally for 8 side triangles.

Border fabric:

11 strips, each 8½" wide, cut on the crosswise grain and pieced to required lengths
OR
4 strips, each 8½" wide, cut on the lengthwise grain for unpieced borders.

Directions

Star Points

1. Sew strips together to create 4 of each unit shown in the piecing diagram below. Letters indicate the color placement. Offset strips about 2¾". Press seams in the direction of the arrows.

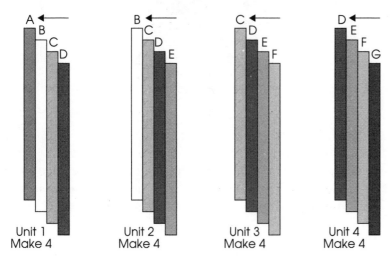

Unit 1
Make 4

Unit 2
Make 4

Unit 3
Make 4

Unit 4
Make 4

2. Follow directions, "Making Secondary Cuts," pages 8–9, to cut each of the units made above into 3"-wide strips. To keep each unit separate, pin a label to each set. Cut 32 strips from each unit.
3. Refer to "Assembling Diamonds," pages 9–10, and as shown at right to assemble 32 star points.

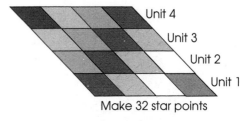

Unit 4
Unit 3
Unit 2
Unit 1

Make 32 star points

Quilt Top Assembly

Refer to pages 10–13, "Assembling Stars" and "Measuring and Inserting Side Triangles and Corner Squares."

1. Using 8 of the pieced diamonds made above, assemble an eight-pointed star.
2. Insert 8 of the 13¼" background squares. In this quilt, do not begin stitching at the edge of outside corner. Instead, begin ¼" from the edge of the corner as shown. This ¼" allowance is necessary to insert the three-star points. Sew to within ¼" of the inside corner. Backstitch carefully at both ends to secure the seam.

    Sew the first side of the square as shown.

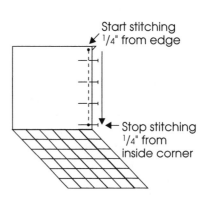

Start stitching ¼" from edge

Stop stitching ¼" from inside corner

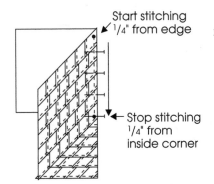

Start stitching ¼" from edge

Stop stitching ¼" from inside corner

Sew the second side of the square as shown. Repeat with the remaining background squares to complete the inner star sections.

Stop stitching ¼" from inside corner

3. Sew 3 star points together. Stitch from the outside edge to within ¼" of the inside corner. Backstitch at the inside corner to secure the seam. Make 8 sets of three-star points.

4. Join the three-star point units to the squares.
   a. Sew one-half of the three-star point to the right-hand side of a square. Start stitching ¼" from the edge and sew to within ¼" from the inside corner. Do not go past the backstitched spot.

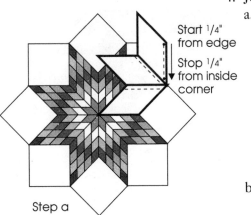

Start ¼" from edge

Stop ¼" from inside corner

Step a

b. Sew the other half of the unit to the adjacent square in the same manner.

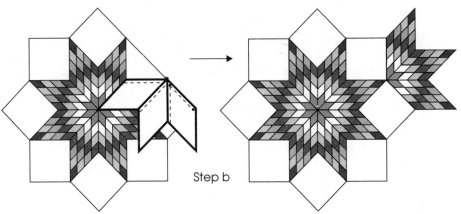

Step b

c. Attach the next three-star point. Sew the seams between the three-star points together. Begin stitching at the outside edge and sew to within ¼" of the inside corner. Do not go past the backstitched spot.

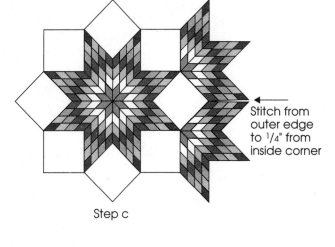

Stitch from outer edge to ¹/₄" from inside corner

Step c

5. Continue around the star until all three-star points are attached.

6. Insert 8 side triangles where indicated by arrows. See page 12 in the "General Instructions."

7. Insert 4 background squares where indicated by arrows. See page 13 in the "General Instructions."

8. Insert 4 corner rectangles as shown to complete the quilt top.

9. I believe a Broken Star doesn't need a fancy border, so I just use background fabric. Measure the quilt top at the centers from raw edge to raw edge and add 16". Cut 8½"-wide border strips to this length and miter corners. (See pages 14–15.) For pieced borders, join 8½"-wide border strips together at the short ends to form one continuous border strip. Cut border strips to required lengths for quilt top.

Finishing

1. Mark top for quilting.
2. Layer with batting and backing; quilt.
3. Bind edges with bias strips of fabric.

Alabama Star

Color photo:
page 34

Quilt size:
Twin (6 blocks) 72" x 102"
King (9 blocks) 102" x 102"

Materials: 44"-wide fabric
See color key below

	Twin	King
Fabric A:	½ yd.	¾ yd.
Fabric B:	⅞ yd.	1¼ yds.
Fabric C:	1¼ yds.	1¾ yds.
Fabric D:	⅞ yd.	1¼ yds.
Fabric E:	½ yd.	¾ yd.
Background:	2½ yds.	3½ yds.
Borders:	1⅝ yds.	2 yds.
	(cut crosswise)	
	OR	
	3 yds.	3 yds.
	(cut lengthwise)	
Binding:	1 yd.	1¼ yds.
Backing:	6½ yds.	9½ yds.

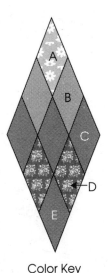

Color Key

Twin ⌐   King ⌐

Cutting

All strips are cut across fabric width (crosswise grain).

From the following fabrics, cut the number of strips given in the widths indicated for the size quilt you are making.

	Strip Width	Number of Strips	
		Twin	King
Fabric A	2½"	5	7
Fabric B	2½"	10	14
Fabric C	2½"	15	21
Fabric D	2½"	10	14
Fabric E	2½"	5	7
Background	9"	6*	9*
	13¼"	2**	3**
*Crosscut these strips into 9" x 9" corner squares. You will need 24 for the Twin- or 36 for the King-size quilt.			
**Crosscut these strips into 13¼" x 13¼" squares. Then cut twice diagonally to make side triangles. You will need 24 triangles for the Twin- or 36 for the King-size quilt.			
Border	6½"	9	11
	(cut crosswise and pieced)		
OR	6½"	4	4
	(cut lengthwise for unpieced border)		

Directions

Star Points

1. Sew strips together to create the number of each unit shown in the piecing diagram at right. Letters indicate the color placement. Offset the strips about 2½". Press the seams in the direction of the arrows.

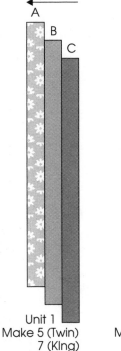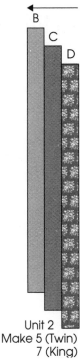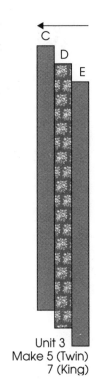

Unit 1
Make 5 (Twin)
7 (King)

Unit 2
Make 5 (Twin)
7 (King)

Unit 3
Make 5 (Twin)
7 (King)

2. Follow directions, "Making Secondary Cuts," pages 8–9, to cut each of the units made above into 2½"-wide strips. To help keep each unit separate, pin a label to each set. Cut a total of 48 strips from each unit for the twin, or a total of 72 strips from each unit for the king.

3. Refer to "Assembling Diamonds," pages 9–10, and the diagram below. Make 48 for the twin and 72 for the king.

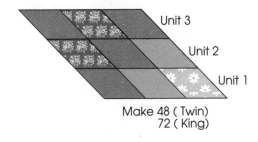

Make 48 (Twin)
72 (King)

Quilt Top Assembly

Refer to pages 10–13, "Assembling Stars" and "Measuring and Inserting Side Triangles and Corner Squares."

1. Using 8 of the pieced diamonds made above for each star, assemble 6 stars for the twin size and 9 stars for the king-size quilt.
2. Measure and insert side triangles and corner squares into each star. Each star block should measure 28½".
3. Assemble quilt top as shown in the quilt plan on page 52.
4. Add borders. (See pages 14–15.)

Finishing

1. Mark top for quilting.
2. Layer with batting and backing; quilt.
3. Bind edges with bias strips of fabric.

Carpenter's Wheel Variation

Color photo:

page 35

Quilt size:

Twin: 65" x 84" (12 blocks)
Full: 84" x 84" (16 blocks)
King: 103" x 103" (25 blocks)

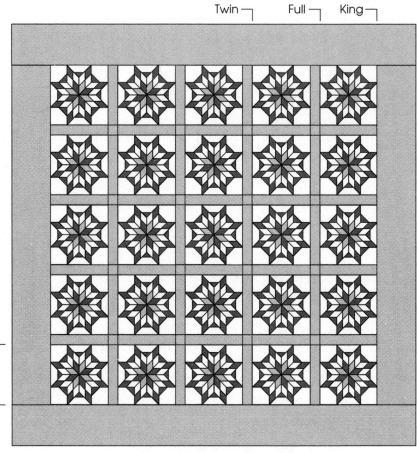

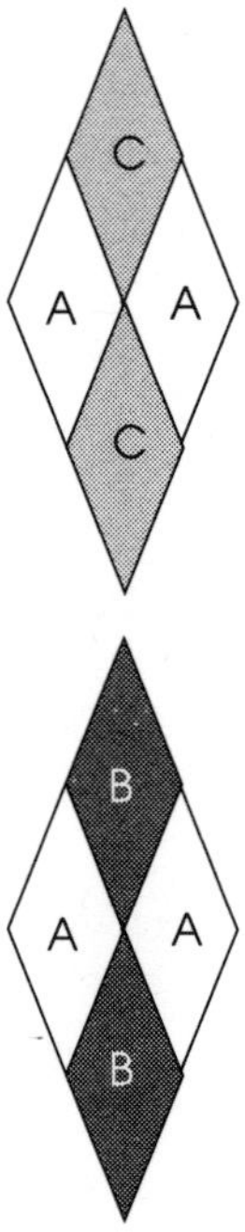

Color Key

Materials: 44"-wide fabric			
See color key at left			
	Twin	**Full**	**King**
Fabric A (Background)	3¼ yds.	4¼ yds.	6½ yds.
Fabric B (Main star)	1½ yds.	2 yds.	3 yds.
Fabric C (Accent star)	⅜ yd.	½ yd.	¾ yd.
Fabric C (Borders and sashing)			
Cut crosswise	2 yds.	2⅜ yds.	3¼ yds.
Cut lengthwise	2½ yds.	2½ yds.	3 yds.
Binding	1 yd.	1 yd.	1¼ yds.
Backing	4 yds.	5¼ yds.	9½ yds.

Cutting

All strips are cut across fabric width (crosswise grain).

From the following fabrics, cut the number of strips given in the widths indicated for the size quilt you are making.

	Strip width	Number of Strips		
		Twin	Full	King
Fabric A (Stars)	2¼"	18	24	38
(Triangles)	5½"	7*	10*	15*
*Crosscut these strips into 5½" x 5½" squares. You will need 48 squares for the Twin-, 64 squares for the Full-, or 100 squares for the King-size quilt.				
(Triangles)	8¼"	3**	4**	7**
**Crosscut these strips into 8¼" x 8¼" squares. You will need 12 squares for the Twin-, 16 squares for the Full-, or 25 squares for the King-size quilt. Then cut the squares twice diagonally for the side triangles. You will need 48 triangles for the Twin-, 64 triangles for the Full-, or 100 triangles for the King-size quilt.				
Fabric B (Stars)	2¼"	13	18	28
(Triangles)	3⅜"	5***	6***	10***
***Crosscut these strips into 3⅜" x 3⅜" squares. You will need 48 squares for the Twin, 64 squares for the Full-, or 100 squares for the King-size quilt. Cut each square once diagonally to make triangles. You will need 96 triangles for the Twin-, 128 triangles for the Full-, or 200 triangles for the King-size quilt.				
Fabric C (Stars)	2¼"	5	6	10
(Sashing)	2½"	10	12	20
		(cut crosswise and pieced)		
OR (Sashing)	2½"	5	6	8
		(cut lengthwise for unpieced sashing)		
(Border)	5½"	8	9	11
		(cut crosswise and pieced)		
OR (Border)	5½"	4	4	4
		(cut lengthwise for unpieced border)		

Directions

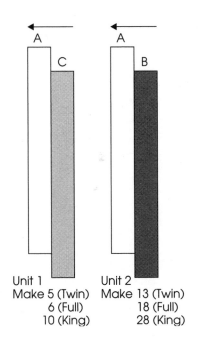

Unit 1
Make 5 (Twin)
6 (Full)
10 (King)

Unit 2
Make 13 (Twin)
18 (Full)
28 (King)

Star Points

1. Using the 2¼" strips of Fabrics A, B, and C, sew strips together to create the number of each unit shown in the piecing diagram at right. Letters indicate the color placement. Offset the strips about 2¼". Press seams in the direction of the arrows.

2. Follow directions, "Making Secondary Cuts," pages 8–9, to make the following units. From Units 1 and 2, cut the number of strips indicated for the size quilt you are making. Cut strips 2¼ " wide.

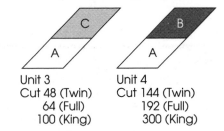

Unit 3
Cut 48 (Twin)
64 (Full)
100 (King)

Unit 4
Cut 144 (Twin)
192 (Full)
300 (King)

3. Sew Unit 3 and Unit 4 to make Unit 5 as shown.

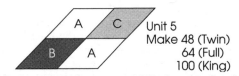

Unit 5
Make 48 (Twin)
64 (Full)
100 (King)

4. Sew 2 Unit 4 strips together to make Unit 6 as shown.

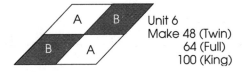

Unit 6
Make 48 (Twin)
64 (Full)
100 (King)

5. Using a 5½" x 5½" square of Fabric A and a 3⅜" half-square triangle of Fabric B, piece the corner squares.

   For each corner square, place a triangle on a square so that the ¼" seam line begins and ends in the corner where the tips of the triangle overlap the edges of the square. Sew ¼" from long edge of triangle and press triangle toward the corner. Corner edge of triangle and square should be even. Do not cut away background fabric.

Make 48 (Twin)
64 (Full)
100 (King)

6. Using a 8¼" quarter-square triangle of Fabric A and a 3⅜" half-square triangle of Fabric B, piece the side triangles.

  For each side triangle, place a small triangle on a large triangle with the long edges of the triangles parallel to each other. Position so the ¼" seam line begins and ends in the corner where the tips of the small triangle overlap the edges of the large triangle. Sew triangles together and press small triangle toward corner. Do not cut away background fabric.

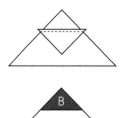

Make 48 (Twin)
64 (Full)
100 (King)

Quilt Top Assembly

Refer to pages 10–13, "Assembling Stars" and "Measuring and Inserting Side Triangles and Corner Squares."

1. Join Unit 5 and Unit 6 in pairs. Join pairs to make half a star, then join halves to make a complete star.
2. Insert pieced corner squares and pieced side triangles for each star. Notice the orientation of the triangle in the corner squares. Completed star blocks should measure 17½" x 17½".
3. From 2½" -wide sashing strips, cut the number of 17½"-long strips indicated below for the sashing between blocks.

Make 12 (Twin)
16 (Full)
25 (King)

Twin	9
Full	12
King	20

  Join blocks in horizontal rows with 17½" sashing strips. Make the number of rows required for desired quilt size. Refer to quilt plan on page 54.

4. Piece the remaining sashing strips together and cut the number of strips in the lengths indicated for the sashing between rows.

Note: It is not necessary to piece strips together if sashing strips were cut from the lengthwise grain of fabric.

Twin	3 strips, each 55½" long
Full	3 strips, each 74½" long
King	4 strips, each 93½" long

5. Join rows together with sashing strips.
6. Add borders. (See pages 14–15.)

Finishing

1. Mark top for quilting.
2. Layer with batting and backing; quilt.
3. Bind edges with bias strips of fabric.

1,000 Pyramids

Color photos:
pages 36 and 37

Quilt size:
Twin 66" x 90"
(52 diamond/triangles)

Queen 84" x 90"
(68 diamond/triangles)

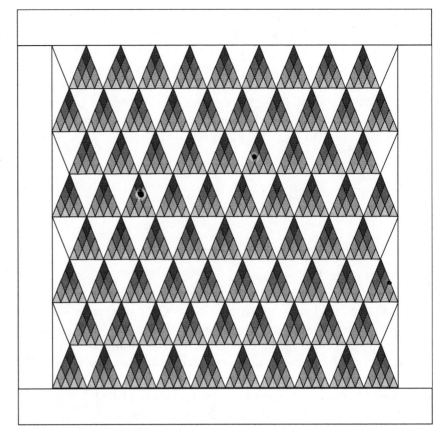

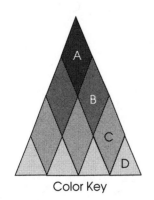

Color Key

Materials: 44"-wide fabric

This quilt is made up of diamond halves. Each diamond half contains a "color set." Each color set contains a dark, medium dark, medium, and light fabric. Each color set makes 10 half diamonds.

Yardage for 1 color set is given in the chart below. For a Twin-size quilt, you will need to purchase fabrics for a total of 6 color sets. For a Queen-size quilt, you will need 7 color sets.

Yardage for One Color Set		
See color key at left	**Twin**	**Queen**
Fabric A (Dark)	⅛ yd.	⅛ yd.
Fabric B (Medium dark)	¼ yd.	¼ yd.
Fabric C (Medium)	⅓ yd.	⅓ yd.
Fabric D (Light)	⅜ yd.	⅜ yd.

Yardage for Background, Border, Backing, and Binding		
Background	4 yds.	5 yds.
Border	1⅝ yds.	1¾ yds.
	(cut crosswise and pieced)	
OR	2¾ yds.	2¾ yds.
	(cut lengthwise for unpieced border)	
Backing	5¾ yds.	5¾ yds.
Binding	¾ yd.	1 yd.

Cutting

All strips are cut across fabric width (crosswise grain).

From each color set, cut the number of 2½"-wide strips indicated for the size quilt you are making.

	Twin	Queen
Fabric A (Dark)	1	1
Fabric B (Medium dark)	2	2
Fabric C (Medium)	3	3
Fabric D (Light)	4	4

From the remaining fabrics, cut the number of strips given in the widths indicated for the size quilt you are making.

	Strip Width	Number of Strips	
		Twin	Queen
Background	8¾"	13	17
	9"	2	2
Border	6½"	8	9
		(cut crosswise and pieced)	
OR	6½"	4	4
		(cut lengthwise for unpieced border)	

Directions

1. Sew the strips from one fabric set together to create 1 of each unit shown in the piecing diagram below. Letters indicate the color placement. Offset the strips about 2½". Repeat for each fabric set. Press seams in the direction of the arrows.

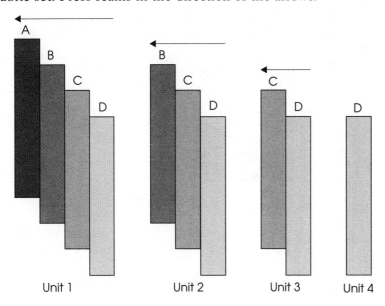

Unit 1   Unit 2   Unit 3   Unit 4

2. Follow directions, "Making Secondary Cuts," pages 8–9, to cut 10 of each unit as shown below. Cut strips 2½" wide.

Note: Unit 4 will be a single diamond when second cut is made.

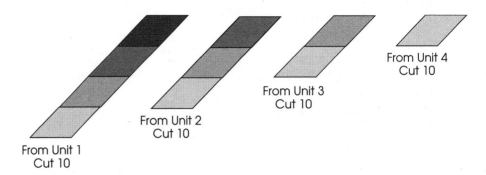

From Unit 1
Cut 10

From Unit 2
Cut 10

From Unit 3
Cut 10

From Unit 4
Cut 10

Repeat for each fabric set.

3. Sew Units 1, 2, 3, and 4 as shown below. Make 10 from each fabric set.

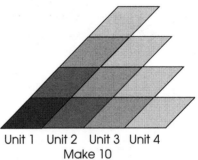

Unit 1   Unit 2   Unit 3   Unit 4
Make 10

4. Place the ¼" mark of the ruler on the end points and at the intersection of the light diamonds as shown. Use your rotary cutter to cut off the ends of the light diamonds. BE SURE TO LEAVE A ¼"-WIDE SEAM ALLOWANCE BEYOND THE FINISHED POINTS OF THE MEDIUM DIAMONDS.

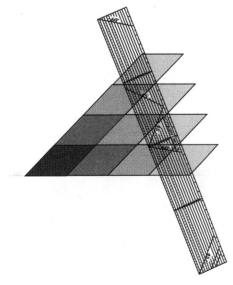

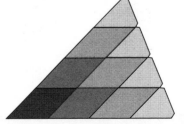

5. Repeat with all the fabric sets.

6. Using the 8¾"-wide strips of background fabric, cut 8¾" diamonds as shown. I use 2 rulers to get the width needed. Cut 34 diamonds.

Cut the diamonds in half crosswise to yield 68 triangles.

7. Using the 9"-wide strips of background fabric, cut 9" diamonds as shown. Cut 4 diamonds.

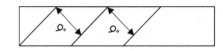

Cut diamonds in half lengthwise to yield 8 side triangles.

Quilt Top Asssembly

1. Arrange in rows, alternating background triangles and pieced half diamonds, as shown in quilt plan on page 58. Do not sew in side triangles yet.
2. Sew rows together.
3. Insert side triangles.
4. Add borders. (See pages 14–15.)

Finishing

1. Mark top for quilting.
2. Layer with batting and backing; quilt.
3. Bind edges with bias strips of fabric.

Polaris Star

Color photo:
page 34

Quilt size:
79" x 100"

Materials: 44"-wide fabric

Small diamonds in star: ⅝ yd.
each of 5 fabrics
OR
40 different strips, each 2" wide

Large diamond in star: 1¾ yds.
Background: 3 yds.

Border: 2¾ yds.
(cut crosswise)
OR
3 yds. (cut lengthwise)

Binding: 1 yd.
Backing: 6 yds.

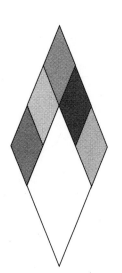

Cutting

All strips are cut across fabric width (crosswise grain).

Fabric for small diamonds:
40 strips, each 2" x 40"

From each of the 5 fabrics for the small diamonds, cut:
8 strips, each 2" wide. If you want to use scrap fabric, cut 1 strip, 2" wide, from each of 40 different fabrics, OR cut 2 strips, each 2" wide, from 20 different fabrics.

Fabric for large diamonds:
14 strips, each 3½" x 40"

Background fabric:

Note: To be on the safe side, you may want to wait until star is asembled to measure and cut corner squares and side triangles.

8 strips, each 7" wide. Crosscut into 48 corner squares, each 7" x 7".

4 strips, each 10½" wide. Crosscut into 12 squares, each 10½" x 10½", and cut twice diagonally for 48 side triangles.

Border fabric:
11 strips, each 8½" wide, cut on the crosswise grain and pieced to required lengths
OR
4 strips, each 8½" wide, cut on the lengthwise grain for unpieced borders.

Directions

Star Points

1. Sew strips together to create the number of each unit shown in the piecing diagram at right. Use fabrics randomly; do not try to match fabrics in units. Notice the different angle of Unit 2. Offset the strips about 2". Press seams in the direction of the arrows.

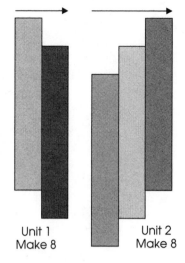

Unit 1
Make 8

Unit 2
Make 8

2. Follow directions, "Making Secondary Cuts," pages 8–9, to make the following units.
   From Unit 1, cut a total of 96 strips, each 2" wide.

Unit 3
Cut 96

From Unit 2, cut a total of 96 strips, each 2" wide. Notice that the 45° angle faces the other way.

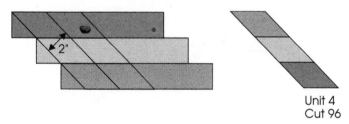

Unit 4
Cut 96

From 3½"-wide strips for large diamonds, cut 96 large diamonds.

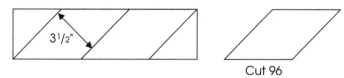

Cut 96

3. Sew Unit 3 to the right side of a large diamond as shown.

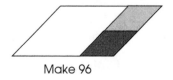

Make 96

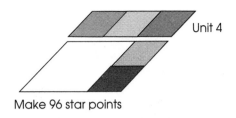
Unit 4

Make 96 star points

4. Sew Unit 4 to the top of the unit assembled in step 3. Do not try to match colors, even if you are using only 5 fabrics.

Quilt Top Assembly

Refer to pages 10–13, "Assembling Stars" and "Measuring and Inserting Side Triangles and Corner Squares."

1. Join 2 pieced diamonds as shown at left. Press seam in the direction of the arrow.

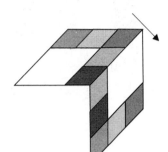

2. Join 4 of the units assembled above to complete a star.

Make 12 stars

3. Measure and insert corner squares and side triangles for each star.
4. Assemble stars in 3 rows of 4 star blocks each.
5. Add borders. (See pages 14–15.)

Finishing

1. Mark top for quilting.
2. Layer with batting and backing; quilt.
3. Bind edges with bias strips of fabric.